G

OF

GOD

JOHN METCALFE

Printed and published by
The Publishing Trust
Tylers Green Chapel, Penn, Buckinghamshire

Copyright 1978
ISBN 0 9502515 9 3
Price 25p

(List of books + order form on page 51)

CONTENTS

THE GOSPEL OF GOD

CONTENTS

THE GOSPEL OF GOD

THE
GOSPEL
OF
GOD

THE APOSTLE PAUL, calling himself a slave of Jesus Christ, was separated unto the Gospel of God. He belonged to it. It was his life. To it, he enchained himself with joy.

Nothing in the world ever had or ever will have firmer foundation than the gospel, nor can anything else compare with its unchangeable durability. From the genesis of holy writing, and for so long as the prophets had spoken, the gospel had been consistently promised and foreshadowed. Now those ancient eras were fulfilled and the everlasting age of the evangel had dawned: what could be more certain? For nothing else was so deeply rooted. Neither could any other doctrine survive the rigours of death, dismissing it with the word of life.

1

The apostle goes on briefly to describe this immutable gospel. In terms of irreducible brevity he defines the evangel as:

> The gospel of God ... ...
> concerning his Son Jesus Christ our Lord,
> which was made of the seed of David
>   according to the flesh;
> and declared to be the Son of God with power,
>   according to the spirit of holiness,
> by the resurrection from the dead.

Epistle to the Romans
Ch. 1 verses 3,4.

What a tremendous summary! But who tells us what it means? Evidently it is a concise definition of the gospel of God, since its brief terms immediately follow the title 'Gospel of God'. And what of that title? This in itself demands our attention. Especially today. So that even before coming to the brief definition which follows, the heading itself challenges modern Christianity. From the beginning of the church the apostle boldly takes his stand, calling out to the end of time. He being dead yet speaketh. In our day we hear the echo of his voice from the one foundation of the church: 'The Gospel of God!' That is his declaration.

This asserts, firstly, that THE GOSPEL IS OF GOD.

Not man. The gospel owes nothing whatever to man. It never was anything to do with men seeking God. It was

2

altogether to do with God seeking men. It is not that the world so loved God that it asked for his Son. It is that God so loved the world that he sent his Son.

The gospel is that body of doctrine which records the exclusive acts of God himself in achieving the salvation of men by Jesus Christ. There is nothing else like it. It is a record of the work of God, Father, Son, and Holy Ghost. It is of God.

The gospel was complete before the church came into existence: indeed its preaching was the means by which the church came into existence. It is still so. The gospel came first. It still comes first. Therefore the gospel borrows nothing whatever from subsequent Christian tradition. How could it? The gospel came first, it came complete, it formed the church, and it is of God.

Even its promulgation is of God. It requires in its very nature that God himself should send out this evangel by grace alone to the hearts of men in each distinct generation throughout the age. The gospel of the grace of God does not depend upon men's religious inclinations in any particular age: it itself gives those inclinations in every age. It is not a matter of men laying hold upon God: it is a matter of God laying hold upon men. The gospel is of God.

The gospel came of God's initiative and it comes of his initiative. It was his doing and it is his doing. What has man got to do with it? It is entirely for men but in no way from them. It is his gospel. That is why it is called 'The Gospel of God'. It is his message to men, upon which they can rely utterly.

3

It is wholly his message; the works of men are nowhere to be found. It is not of works. Neither the ministry nor the church can either add to it or subtract from it: all they can do to the contrary is to adulterate it, obscure it, and misname the result 'gospel': but it is not the gospel. Because the gospel is wholly God's message.

It is his whole message; it is the evangel: to evangelise is therefore to declare the entire range of the truth of the gospel. Otherwise the evangel is eroded, polluted and degraded; however, then the name 'evangelism' becomes meaningless in fact. Just an empty word. But the real gospel never changes.

It is the Lord's last message; he will not speak again till he comes again. The last word has been spoken. And the name of the word is the gospel of God. It is the New Testament. It is summarised in Romans 1:3,4. The gospel is absolutely from God; it is entirely out of heaven; it is everlastingly from eternity. You need have no doubt about resting your whole weight here!

Secondly, THE GOSPEL IS ENTIRELY OF GOD.

From the beginning God brought it in; God wrought it out; God set it forth; and God ordained both its preachers and its preaching. There was never any thought of sharing or delegating any of these divine prerogatives to men. Otherwise it would not be entirely of God. But the gospel is entirely of God, from God, and by God. In it he has fully revealed himself, and to it he confines that revelation. It is by the gospel and by the gospel alone that God is made known: but there he is made known entirely.

4

The gospel is entirely of God: it has his stamp, seal, hallmark and character. No other doctrine in heaven or earth has this authenticity. God's authority is behind it; his initiative protects it; his word opens it; his majesty upholds it; his Son commands it; and his Spirit attends it. Therefore the gospel is superior to the apostles; superior to the ministry; superior to the church; and superior to evangelism. Only the gospel can give these things their true character, as Judas found to his cost at Jerusalem, Peter to his shame at Galatia, Demas to his disgrace at Thessalonica, and the seven churches to their peril in Revelation.

Because the gospel is entirely of God it is attended and characterised by God, Almighty God, by God and the Father. It does not stop short with the Holy Spirit, or even emphasise the Spirit, although the outpouring of the Spirit is given to the hearing of faith. It does not stop short with the Son, although the person and work of the Son of God is the subject of the gospel. Nevertheless the gospel is not a declaration of how we are brought to Christ, but how he brings us to the Father. The Son is not the interceptor between God and men: he is the mediator between God and men. If so, he brings men to God. And he does it by the gospel.

Therefore the presence and fear of God himself distinguish those who receive and obey the gospel. It is unmistakable. They worship God and the Father. Anything else at all indicates that less than the gospel has been preached, or more than the gospel added. For the gospel brings into the very presence of God and the Father. It must do. It is the gospel of God. And it is entirely of God.

5

Thirdly, THE GOSPEL IS ENTIRE IN ITSELF.

The English translation 'gospel' — or transliteration 'ev-angel' — answers to the New Testament Greek εὐαγγέλιον, *euaggelion*, phonetically pronounced 'evangel-ion'. This compound Greek word is comprised of *aggelion*, the Greek for *message*, and the prefix *eu*, as qualifying that message. The qualifying prefix possesses quite a wide range of meaning, but always carries the underlying idea of *well, nobly, in good case, well-disposed*.

However the meaning of *eu* — as qualifying the 'angelion', *message* — may reach to the thought of *thoroughly* well, leaving no stone unturned, no untouched corners: everything has been faced, nothing under the carpet, all is done properly and thoroughly: well done! Another application of *eu* — qualifying the 'angelion', *message* — is that of *competently* well, in the sense of being of power, able, suited, having competence: well able! From this it is obvious that the mere 'glad' or even 'good' will not do in this context to qualify the message.

Besides, whatever the precise bearing of *'eu'*, the word *message* — ἀγγέλιον — certainly can never mean mere 'tidings', much less 'news'. Which the 'glad tidings' and 'good news' enthusiasts may desire but cannot translate. Both 'tidings' and 'news' are transient in their essence and of necessity soon become old-fashioned and stale. This cannot happen to the everlasting gospel and it is certainly not the translation of *angelion*, *message*.

In the gospel God has come down to men: the glory of God appears. God has spoken, and spoken in his Son. That is the nature of the message. The message itself is integral, entire, complete. Everything about it, even the means by which it is propagated, all is within itself. *It* is the power of God unto salvation. Nothing else is needed. No 'new methods' are needed. It is entire within itself; it is all of God's initiative from beginning to end, and absolutely no assistance from outside is required.

Grace is not of works. Otherwise grace is no more grace. But the gospel is of grace. God will do it all, or nothing will be done. Not for eternity.

Occurring — in one form or another — over one hundred times in the New Testament, the word 'gospel' signifies the message of the God of all grace to mankind. But if message, then *content* is implied. A message is to be delivered to the addressee just as it was dispatched by the sender. If it is tampered with it is no longer the original message. For the gospel to be the gospel of God it must be delivered entire and intact to men.

. God's message is not subject to man's opinion, guesswork, alteration, ignorance, 'scholarship', interpretation, addition, subtraction, division; what is required is that it should in fact be delivered. And if so, by the messengers chosen and commissioned by the sender.

The apostles were not in this sense authors, but messengers of the author. It is God that has spoken, not them. Theirs was to deliver from him to men the thing that he had said. The message was, and is, to be conveyed exactly as delivered. And not the least reason for this is, that the gospel is entire within itself.

Fourthly, THE GOSPEL IS PREACHED.

The gospel of God cannot be conveyed but by preaching and teaching. How could it? It is a *message*, not an influence. Almighty God has ordained the knowledge of his Son, of himself, of his salvation, and of the giving of his Spirit *through preaching and teaching.* The apostle states in Romans 1:15, I am ready to *preach* the gospel to you. And again, 6:17, Ye have obeyed from the heart that *form of doctrine* which was *delivered* you. Once more, 10:14, How shall they hear without a *preacher?* The apostolic ministry was exclusive to preaching and teaching. By no other means was the gospel conveyed to the New Testament church.

Whatever signs, wonders and miracles attended Jesus' ministry, it was preaching itself that constituted that ministry. To preach and teach was the essence of the apostolic commission. It was the method of the early church. And it is the heritage of all spiritual ministry.

Moreover the kind of preaching to which we refer can only be fulfilled by those chosen of God, called of Christ, prepared by the Spirit, and sent from heaven for the purpose. Now: Christians may and should testify of their experience and this is good; but it is not to be confused with this sent ministry. Also: brethren may and should speak according to the oracles of God and that is right; but it is not to be confused with this sent ministry. Again: saints with gifts of the Spirit in the assembly should minister as of the sufficiency which God giveth and that is proper; but it is not to be confused with this sent ministry.

Such a ministry, called of God, ordained of Christ, and

sent by the Spirit, is directed into all the world and to every creature. It is sent to the whole church, every assembly, and all saints. And it comes from God not man, Christ not the church, heaven not earth, and is in the power of the Spirit not the deadness of the letter. The preparation of such an anointed ministry is divine not scholastic; prophetic not pedantic; spiritual not academic; and providential not financial.

This is what is needed, sore needed and needed desperately to restore and revive gospel preaching in every locality today. Only this can but this does bring in the effectual and mighty growth of the word of God. 'So mightily grew the word of God and prevailed.' 'The Lord gave the word: great was the company of those that published it.' It is this that encourages all the assemblies and makes every grace within the congregation to flourish and prosper.

There is no alternative to such a ministry for the upholding and advancement of Christ's interests, for the defence and maintenance of the gospel, and for the revival and recovery of the church. It is the criterion of spiritual life. Without this everything decays and lapses into apathy and deadness. Worldly corruption and the sleep of death prevail. A vast host of idolatrous inventions and practices appear. Instead of days of heaven upon earth there is a state of indifferent inertia; unbelieving despair crushes the spirit, and the plague of dissolution seems irremediable.

Without that Christ raises up and sends down such a ministry we are undone. Absolutely no substitute exists or can exist for this heaven-sent anointed ministry. No substitute form of ministry can have any apostolic, scriptural,

9

doctrinal or spiritual authority for its existence. Let alone its actually taking the place of the sole preaching of the gospel by that ministry sent from Christ for the purpose.

Does one ask, How shall we know such ministers? I answer, by those very same virtues, sufferings, providences, and persecutions that distinguished the New Testament ministry of which we read and of whom they are the true successors. By the love of the brethren, by the hatred of the hirelings, by the simplicity of their bearing, by their fruits ye shall know them.

By their manifestation of the truth, by their agreement with the doctrine, by comparing their word and spirit with the word and spirit of the prophets, apostles, and New Testament ministers in the Bible. Yes, and by their fearing God and not men; serving Christ and not churches; seeing things invisible and not visible: oh, be assured, we shall not mistake them. There is no mistaking them.

Theirs is the ministry. And this is the means by which God has chosen to save sinners, remit sins, impute righteousness, bring in the believer, sanctify the saints, form the church, edify the body, build up the house, supply the Spirit, impart the Son, unite with the Father, and prepare for glory. That is, by the gospel of God in the mouth of those sent to revive it in their own generation.

Now, fifthly, THE GOSPEL IMPARTS CHRIST.

Nothing is more important than to grasp that it is through the gospel itself that Christ is imparted and only through the gospel. The gospel is the cause of Christ's being imparted. There are many effects from this cause but Christ is not imparted through any of them. Solely through the gospel itself.

For instance, the gospel effected the apostle Peter's conversion. But to convert others, the apostle did not preach his own conversion: he preached what caused it: he preached the gospel. None of the apostles preached his own conversion: they preached what actually converted them: the gospel itself. And this is true of every New Testament minister. 'Philip preached *Christ* unto them.'

Paul did not preach his own testimony. He preached GOD'S testimony. His own testimony was what God had done for him. But God's testimony was what God had done to his own Son. Salvation is through faith in the gospel, the testimony of God concerning his Son. That was what transformed the early believers.

The objective truth of the gospel was the cause: conversion was the effect. The gospel of God itself made the difference. That was what Paul preached.

In fact Paul's full testimony is recorded only three times, and all in Acts. The first time it is the narrative of the event by Luke. The other occasions both record Paul himself giving his testimony, but then he is not preaching: in each case the apostle is defending himself before his judges. Yet if Paul's personal testimony occurs only three times, *the gospel of God* which was the cause of that testimony occurs as the constant and uniform subject of every epistle.

Paul did not preach his own spiritual blessings, gifts,

ecstasies, experiences. They could not impart Christ to others: only the gospel itself could do that.

Yet Paul had visions, revelations, ecstasies and experiences beyond tongue to tell or lawful word to utter. He could write of one being caught up to the third heaven, transported into a realm unspeakable. He could; but he did not. We know of the incident only because Paul was provoked by the Corinthians' lack of confidence in him, favouring those who were without call or experience in Christ. Paul mentions this vision but once; he does not actually say it was himself, simply 'I knew a man in Christ' II Cor. 12:1-4. When finally he speaks, it is some fourteen years after the event. Yet Paul had preached at Corinth continually for over one and a half years, had written to them, and sent his ministers to them. Nevertheless, over all those years he never mentioned this transport to heaven. Not until the end of the second epistle. Then as provoked. And no reference to the matter occurs in any other epistle.

No, Paul did not preach his own experiences: he preached the gospel. Nothing else could save men. Nothing else could impart Christ.

The consequences of believing the gospel brought together the saints in the church or assembly, singing praises, testifying of spiritual experiences, in exhortations, in worship, and in all manner of meetings. And if this assembling, those experiences and such meetings proved to be sound and spiritual — which was by no means always the case, as the corrective epistles show — well. Excellent. Doubtless there was a real measure of profit from all those things — rightly fulfilled — in their proper place. But they are no substitute for the preaching and teaching of the doctrine of the gospel!

No testimony, neither singing, nor yet praising; no experience, neither open meeting, nor worship service actually imparts Christ. Rather these things are the effect of his having been imparted already. As if to say, in effect, Christ has been given for us, imparted to us, is in communion with us, and this is the effect upon us. But this effect is not the cause. The sole cause which produced that effect is the gospel. It is only the gospel itself which actually achieves that giving, imparting, and communicating of Christ. Solely the gospel.

Therefore nothing — but nothing — else was is or ever can be a substitute for the gospel. It, and it alone, is the power of God unto salvation.

This applies universally; no matter what area, irrespective of however wonderful, profound and varied, heavenly and glorious, the effects of the gospel of God. They are not the gospel itself. They are caused by the gospel itself. They are the effects, or the signs of the effects, or the result of its being effectual. This is true in the individual and in the church. It is true of conversions, it is true of ministry, it is true of ordinances, it is true of baptism, it is true of worship, it is true of the Lord's Supper, it is true of church government and discipline.

All these things are consequential, they are the effects, the subjective or objective marks or signs of an individual or church having received the gospel. But they are not the gospel itself. And only the gospel imparts Christ. It, and it alone, is the power of God unto salvation.

No wonder it is called the 'gospel of God'. No wonder we are required to understand what the apostle means:

First, that the gospel is of God;
Second, that the gospel is entirely of God;
Third, that the gospel is entire in itself;
Fourth, that the gospel is preached;
and Fifth, that the gospel imparts Christ.

No wonder! To what man or body of men would God delegate such incalculably priceless doctrine? None at all. The first covenant failed precisely because it was entrusted to a succession of men. However the new covenant succeeds because it is retained in the hands of God. The gospel is of God. God has retained it in his own hands. The Father has put it into the hands of the everlasting Son.

And that is where it stays. The gospel is of God. He gave it; he dispenses it; he conveys it; he ordains its preaching. So that the sum of our apostolic doctrine is seen to be contained in these four principles:

1. THE GOSPEL IMPARTS CHRIST AND NOTHING ELSE DOES.

2. PREACHING AND TEACHING CONVEY THE GOSPEL AND NOTHING ELSE DOES.

3. CHRIST SENDS THE PREACHERS AND TEACHERS AND NO ONE ELSE CAN.

4. THIS MINISTRY IS SENT DIRECTLY TO THE WORLD
   AND GIVEN STRAIGHT TO THE CHURCH WITHOUT
   INTERMEDIARIES.

These four principles are derived from the grace of God,
and they are conveyed to the faith of believers. And so it is
that we have deduced the sum of the doctrine.

Now it is our duty to turn to its enemies and show how
they seek to overturn the gospel of God, to confound its
four cardinal principles, and confuse the truth that it is
derived from grace and received by faith.

But who would dare deny that only the gospel imparts
Christ? When did any ever dream of opposing the principle
that only preaching and teaching convey the gospel? Where
on earth shall they be found who would deny that Christ
authorises the ministry and Christ alone? How could
men frustrate the grace of God by denying the world
such evangelists, or shutting out such ministers from the
professing church? Who? When? Where? How?

Who? Well, for example, the Anglican-Roman Catholic
Commission which met to make the Agreed Statements on
the Eucharist, the Ministry, and on Authority. When? In
1971, 1973, and in 1976 respectively. Where? First at
Windsor; next at Canterbury; finally in Venice. How? How
do these three papers contradict our apostolic and gospel
principles? Because effectively they shut out by conscience
on the one hand and by rejection on the other, the heavenly
ministry sent by Christ for men's salvation.

How? By conscience: that is, the grieved conscience of

15

godly and righteous men of God. By rejection: because since the ministry defined by the Commission is so contrary to that sent by Christ, they find no more room for them than did disobedient Israel for the faithful prophets sent to deliver the people from the lies of their leaders.

How?

1. BY ASSERTING (Windsor 1971) THAT IT IS THE EUCHARIST WHICH IMPARTS CHRIST.

2. BY TEACHING THAT SINCE THE WAY IN WHICH CHRIST IS IMPARTED IS SACRAMENTAL, THEN THE CHARACTER OF THE MINISTRY MUST BE PRIESTLY AND SACRIFICIAL (Canterbury 1973).

3. BY SUBMITTING THAT THE AUTHORITY FOR THAT MINISTRY (Venice 1976) IS DERIVED FROM 'THE FIRST BISHOP OF ROME' CENTRED AT THE VATICAN.

Now, we used to know of the Roman Sacrifice as the Mass. But the Roman Catholics have agreed to change the name alone, and the Anglicans have stated that they will consider the unaltered reality under the new agreed term 'Eucharist'.

And we used to know the name of the Vatican Hierarchy as the Roman Priesthood, but now it appears that exactly the same thing will be agreeable to the Anglican clergy under the new term 'Ministry'.

And we used to call the 'first bishop of Rome' as the

Pope. But now, with the adjusted title, the agreed statement allows that both communions together may accept the 'first bishop of Rome' in practice as the one Head of the body, the Church.

And we used to believe that Christ, when he ascended up on high, himself gave some apostles, some prophets, and continues to give some evangelists, some pastors and teachers. But now we are required to acquiesce that Christ has delegated his prerogative to 'the first bishop of Rome', and that we are no longer expected to look up to heaven for the ministry because from henceforth Italy is to command our gaze.

This defies with precision the apostolic doctrine of the gospel, exactly in its four cardinal principles. First, that Christ is imparted through the gospel alone, not the 'sacraments' at all. Second, that the character of the ministry is doctrinal and the very opposite to all that is sacerdotal. Third, that authority is retained in Christ and in nowise delegated to the 'first bishop' of Rome. And finally, that authority is dispensed from heaven throughout the age: never is any geographical location elevated in the New Testament. Were it, Jerusalem might be the favoured choice. Certainly not Italy. But heaven is the divine direction.

The authority of the Son of God from heaven makes appeal to the judgment of the congregation not the hierarchy of the bishops. And the expression of that authority is the gospel of God — the true keys of the kingdom — not the church or the 'sacraments'. Even supposing that it were the gospel that brought in the church and 'sacraments' under consideration.

17

And who supposes that? Well, the three agreed statements suppose it. They suppose that both Roman Catholic
and Anglican communions are justified by the gospel. But
before such a presupposition can be considered valid, the
gospel must be elevated. Both communions and the terms
of their union must be tried by the gospel. Yet the truth is,
the host is elevated, rather than the gospel.

Now, the hub of the matter is this: How are the merits
of Christ's work on Calvary conveyed to the faithful? They
are saying, individually and together, by the sacrament
of the Eucharist; through the ministry of one ordained
priesthood; deriving authority from the first bishop of
Rome.

But that was what Roman Catholics have always said,
and to which tenaciously they have always clung; it was this
obstinate unyieldingness that forced the division when
multitudes cried out for reform. That reformation from
those Roman errors gendered the Church of England. Now,
they return to what Rome has consistently maintained.
Effectively, this dissolves the Church of England in its
original character. Nevertheless we re-state what the Church
of England began stating four hundred years ago — which
brought it into distinctive existence — *that Christ's merits
are conveyed by faith through the gospel alone.*

Yet in these papers nothing is more conspicuous by its
absence than this cardinal article of the church. In truth,
the gospel is missing; and the Church of England properly
so-called is missing also! In the Agreement, all roads lead
to Rome and none to the gospel. To disguise this retreat —
which falling numbers, closing churches, dwindling revenues,

18

diminishing clergy, and universal contempt in the name of science threaten to turn into a rout — I say, to disguise this retreat, there is the pretence of much biblical language and conception, some of which reaches excellence: but NONE OF WHICH DESCRIBES EITHER THE TWO PARTIES OR WHAT IS ACTUALLY GOING ON!

Much scripture is quoted; apostolic positions are defined. But what is actually taking place behind this smoke-screen is a full-scale about turn in which the modern Church of England effectively denies the Reformation and really retreats from the scriptural advance so far made by it. Meanwhile, Rome stands still. And the gospel remains ignored.

Then what of the gospel? The Commission is acting upon the unfounded, untried, and untrue assumption that both Church of England and Roman Catholic communions are necessarily gospel churches. But the position of the Reformation and of the Church of England until comparatively recently, was that the Roman Catholic communion was not and is not a gospel church. Well then, by this definition, neither is that which submits to its sacrifice, hierarchy, and authority.

Truly we stand aside to see this great wonder, and say to that Rome which in times past Church of England bishops, archbishops, clergy and their long-venerated canons have called antichrist and a harlot — even the mother of harlots! — and we say to her now: 'Woman, where are those thine accusers?'

For the children of those accusers now propose to join

the accused whom their fathers condemned, thus making themselves one. Moreover the children are doing so under the guise of biblical quotes on the church, on ministry, and on authority, bearing no relation whatsoever to either of the two bodies or to what they are doing in fact. Besides, what has happened to the old biblical quotations of the fathers used to justify separation from Rome? The new texts sprinkled by the commission look good. But they are all dust in the eyes. Irrelevant, immaterial and completely beside the point.

But a word brings it all to light: THE GOSPEL COMES FIRST.

These things being so, 'What meaneth then this bleating of the sheep in mine ears, and the lowing of the oxen which I hear? Hath the LORD as great delight in burnt offerings and sacrifices, as in obeying the voice of the LORD? Behold, to obey is better than sacrifice, and to hearken than the fat of rams. For rebellion is as the sin of witchcraft, and stubbornness is as iniquity and idolatry. Because thou hast rejected the word of the LORD, he hath also rejected thee from being king.' I Samuel 15.

But what of the church? Is it that we do not understand the nature of the church, nor the earnest desires of the Anglican-Roman Catholic Committee to put away division and recover visible unity? Have we no vision of the church?

But have they no vision of the church? For how can they understand the nature of the church, who accept *carte blanche* the *status quo* of each of the existing denominations as if nothing were intrinsically wrong, and as if the sum of them were the very same thing as the church in the New Testament, save divided?

As if no more were needed than that all independent halls should be absorbed by the Free Church denominations, all the Free Church denominations should then be incorporated within the Church of England, and finally the whole should be embraced within the fold of a real catholicism. Nevertheless, Roman Catholicism.

Would then division be swallowed up of unity? No it would not: it would be a purely political solution, and not in any way a spiritual one. It would be nothing more than man's engineering and worldly manipulation with existing parties. But we are supposed to be talking about the church of God.

Then what is God's solution? Why, I have kept telling you: the gospel of God, of course.

That comes first.

But we who say this, are we so preoccupied with the gospel, that by it we obscure the church? Do we have no vision of the church? Is that the case? God forbid.

The word of the Lord and the testimony of our conscience teach us that we must not obscure our heavenly vision by being infatuated with earthly institutions. We are not to allow the divine and spiritual revelation of the church to be submerged beneath the historical tide of existent systems. Otherwise we should be guilty of endorsing without gospel authority or heavenly witness what is no more than a worldly substitute for the true church. A substitute, I would add, dangerously near those dreadful prophecies of Christ and the apostles as to what the heirs of organised Christendom should inherit in the last days.

So just who are the ones without vision? We dreamers? I think not. God knoweth. Many may judge that we are without vision of the church, the ministry, or of authority. But conscience tells us that they are wrong. Judgment declares boldly that it is they who have no vision, because — whereas we start with nothing but vision — they start by accepting what the natural eye can see.

That is, they start by accepting intact and without question the existing and separate organisations of Christendom, with these to mould their ideal by the schemes and works of their subtle politic.

One church! they cry with apparent idealism, one church, having many local manifestations. One ministry! they declare with seeming meekness, one ministry, setting forth that church's order. One authority! they proclaim with evangelical fervour, one authority to end all strife and discord.

Yes, apparent idealism. But to achieve it, they do not judge themselves by the gospel. They will not repent and remove all that man has already imposed upon God's church. They do not fall on their faces, and cry for God to do what they cannot. No. They take up things as they are, and do what they please, on the one hand conspicuously ignoring the gospel of God and on the other putting their confidence in the works of their own hands.

22

What shall we then say to these things? Heart-broken we weep, Lord, I have sinned and thy people. We groan with spiritual groanings that cannot be uttered. And for what cause?

Because we have a heavenly vision of one body, under the headship and authority of Christ. Each local manifestation of that body one with the body. One Spirit and one calling. One Lord, one faith, one baptism. One God and Father of all, above all, through all and in all.

We have a heavenly vision of a ministry sent down from the ascended Son of God. Sent to perfect the saints, sent for the work of the ministry in the assembly, sent for the edifying of the body of Christ. A ministry received by all, a visible expression of our unity.

Yes, we have the vision. That is what we see in the Spirit. What to us the splits, splinters, sects, denominations, federations, independencies, individual missions, mighty state churches, and historical edifices? 'Well' they cry in triumph, 'You with your vision! Where are you in fact?'

Oh, we weep in contrition, we are not, for the Lord hath chastened us sore; he hath bitterly afflicted his people. He hath shut up his wretched servants in prison: we are cast into the pit where no water is. That is true. Where is our vision? That we can describe to you. Where is the reality? Alas, we can but weep and wring our hands mutely. But for all that, we will neither submit, agree, join, nor be confederate with this worldly substitute for the heavenly reality, this human counterfeit for what nothing but the hand of God can raise up by grace alone through the gospel.

But then suppose, suppose, suppose that as in times past the Lord should be pleased to turn our captivity; that he should visit his people in giving them bread; that he should be pleased to wash away all our filth and throughly purge away all our iniquity. What if the Lord should turn to himself a people having a pure language: that he should gather that people in the Spirit: at last bringing a penitent remnant into the unity of one body unto spiritual Mount Zion, to the Father's house. What then?

Then, my brethren, then, for all that, even so much blessedness would not impart Christ. It would impart blessedness. But like the manna of old, it will not keep past the day: it is not for tomorrow: and it is not the Giver but the gift. Were the Lord to command our assembly again, such a unity would be a long-neglected, long wept-for, long cried-after effect of the gospel. After so long a time. Indeed, in this present world, such a unity would be the final, the ultimate effect of the gospel. Nevertheless, not even this blessedness would in and of itself impart Christ; it would be the effect of his having been blissfully imparted. But the imparting itself is through the gospel and the gospel alone. Only the gospel imparts Christ.

Now therefore let this all-important saying sink down in your ears. The apostles did not confuse or confound cause and effect. They knew what caused the salvation of sinners, the sanctification of saints, the edification of the body, and the bringing in of the church. They knew the cause whereby Christ was imparted and the Spirit given, both to the believing individual and the faithful congregation. It was the preaching of the gospel, the whole gospel, and nothing but the gospel. This produced blessed and heavenly effects in the penitent, the sanctified, and in the Spirit-filled assembly of God's people. That was why the apostles and prophets preached the gospel. Because it was the cause of Christ's being imparted.

And yet today we have all but lost this singular cause under a proliferation of effects, some of them with a vaguely scriptural origin but many of them borrowed from the world or invented. Indeed, modern Christianity is full of things that never occurred to or in the early church. For the early church was raised up through the preaching of the gospel, neither more nor less. The gospel did its own work, it produced its own results. All the effects of that preaching followed of their own accord.

That is why it is so damaging to be diverted from the touchstone of the gospel itself, whether through the question of authority, the ministry, or of the church. Or any other question whatsoever. Since under the apostles these things followed from the preaching of the gospel, then they are not questions in and of themselves to be isolated from it. On the contrary, they can only be resolved by determining their relationship to the gospel.

The ministry is not the gospel: it exists for the gospel. Authority is not distinct from the gospel: it is within the gospel. The church is not the gospel: it is caused by the gospel. The gospel is the criterion for all these questions. The Spirit is not given but under the gospel. Christ is not imparted but through the gospel. The Father is not known but in the gospel. The Bible is not understood but with the gospel. And salvation would never have been given but for the gospel.

Once elevate the gospel and all these things appear in their true colours and their proportionate context: it is the gospel that determines these questions. But once obliterate the gospel and nothing is left but a trackless wilderness; an endless maze; a treacherous sand where there is no standing.

But we are beset about today with so many effects, some of them with a nominal biblical connection, but most of them substitutes and innovations. By these the apostolic preaching of the truth has been first diminished, then obscured, and finally presumed superfluous.

For the clear clean doctrine of the gospel — which should judge everything — has been buried beneath a welter of effects.

It has been submerged beneath the ever-rising tide of Christendom, of traditions, evangelisms, conventions, singing and entertainments, baptisms, forms of government, no church government at all, ministry, no ministry at all, state aided ministerial training, state paid ministerial trainers, suppers, eucharists, communions, unions, creeds, breaking bread, gifts, charisma, blessings, second blessings, promises, books, tracts, records, tapes, Christian leisure, Christian tours, Christian holidays, fellowships, societies, sacred concerts, music of all sorts, experiences, healings, meetings, youth exploitation, groups, Sunday schools, discussions, solos, monetary schemes, charities, movements of every kind, missions of all sorts, missionary societies, free churches, Anglican churches, Catholic churches, no churches at all. Oh, what a welter, what a confusion, of effects true and false!

Yet in the beginning there was one church, one congregation, and a total economy and absolute simplicity of gospel orderliness. Maybe. But however can one find one's way today? Easily. Since all these things are but the effects, or the claimed effects, then the raising up of the doctrine of the gospel immediately acts as a watershed.

With Almighty God, the gospel is the sole cause of all that he effects or ever authorises in the church. Anything else is spurious, no matter what the extent of its acceptance, no matter what the pretension of its claims, and no matter what its real or supposed antiquity. The preaching of the gospel is the sole cause and its teaching the only maintenance of all that is truly of God. By it alone, he imparts, conveys, and communicates his Son.

Sixthly then, NOTHING BUT THE GOSPEL IMPARTS CHRIST.

By the gospel — the keys of the kingdom — Christ is glorified before, united within and imparted unto his people in a spiritual way. There is but one exercise that secures the gospel to his people: faith. Not the faith of the ministry or in it. Neither the faith of the church or in it. Nor the faith of any one or number of persons acting for another, whether in or out of the church. But the faith of the individual particularly and in the gospel exclusively.

Now faith comes by hearing and hearing only. And hearing by the word of God and the word of God alone. And the word of God by preaching and solely by preaching. The apostle insists upon this in the Epistle to the Romans Ch. 10:14-17. So does the Lord Jesus in the parable of the sower: 'The sower soweth *the word.*' 'Now the parable is this: the seed is *the word of God.*' 'They should *believe* and be saved.'

Therefore there is absolutely no way other than by faith. No way other than through hearing the faithful preaching of the word of God. No way other than by believing the doctrine of the gospel as delivered by the Lord Jesus and his holy apostles. Absolutely no way. No way other than by the way of faith in order to:

> Receive the merits of Christ's death. Eat of his flesh and drink of his blood. Enter into interior union and communion with his person. Be united with and incorporated into his body. Dwell in him and he in us. No way, but by faith through the preaching of the gospel.

> Be regenerate and baptised with the Holy Ghost. Enter into the inward communion of the Holy Ghost. Drink into one Spirit. Be filled with the Spirit. Receive of his gifts and blessings. Be sealed under his ministry. No way, but by the hearing of faith in the word of the truth of the gospel.

> Be one with the Father. Have the Spirit of sonship crying from within, Abba, Father. Become his interior and holy temple in the Lord. Have the love of God shed abroad in our hearts. Be filled with all the

fulness of God. Dwell in God. Enter into
the oneness of the Father and the Son. Be
made partaker of the divine nature.

No way, but by believing the gospel of God concerning his
Son.

Now then, as to this knowledge of the Father, the Son,
and the Holy Ghost, here are three momentous principles:

1. IT IS BY THE GOSPEL AND BY THE GOSPEL
   ALONE.

2. IT IS THROUGH FAITH, AND THROUGH FAITH
   ONLY.

3. FAITH IS BY THE RATIONAL HEARING OF THE
   INTELLIGIBLE PREACHING OF THE WORD OF
   GOD.

But then, these things being so, and moreover indis-
putably so, how can one account for the following words
spoken over a helpless and unreasoning baby? An infant
incapable of speech, proper hearing, of voluntary move-
ment, thought, and even conception? A total dependant?
Non-rational, not accountable, without obligation, having
neither capability nor awareness? An innocent suckling, an
oblivious infant of a few days unable to form a word, a
thought, an idea?

> 'Then the Priest shall say: "Sanctify this
> water to the mystical washing away of
> sin."

29

'Then the Priest shall dip it in the water
discreetly and warily.'
'Then the Priest do sign him with the sign
of the cross ... and say:

"Seeing now that this child is regenerate,
"and grafted into the body of Christ's
"church ... it hath pleased thee to regen-
"erate this infant." '

Seeing *now?* That this child is *what?*

Sanctify this *water?* To wash away *sin?* In an uncomprehending new-born *infant?* What medieval darkness is this?

What *are* they talking about? Have they never heard?

1. IT IS BY THE GOSPEL AND BY THE GOSPEL
   ALONE.

2. IT IS THROUGH FAITH AND FAITH ONLY.

3. IT IS BY FAITH OF THE RATIONAL INDIVIDUAL
   AND THROUGH THE INTELLIGIBLE PREACHING
   OF THE WORD OF GOD.

Yes, they have heard, for the same Prayer Book as that
in which the Baptismal Regeneration formula occurs also
contains the thirty-nine Articles, the ninth of which states
'That we are justified by faith only is a most wholesome
doctrine.' 'Justified by faith *only*' notice. But the infant
whose 'baptism' we have quoted was not justified by faith.
He was justified by water: 'Sanctify this *water* to the

washing away of sin.' If so, he was justified by water only, and not by faith at all.

Indeed, in the case of this Baptismal Justification there was no faith; no gospel; no preacher; no hearing and no rational individuality. Whereas in the case of the ninth article there is faith only; therefore the gospel; hence preaching; and consequently hearing; and necessarily rational understanding. Now, how can these two things subsist together?

They cannot. They are contradictory. They are mutually exclusive. Then what are they doing in the same Prayer Book? In a book with such wholesome doctrine as the ninth article, whence came this corrupt ritual? It is nothing but a superstitious fable completely in opposition to the faith of the gospel expressed in the Article on Justification. But if so, why did not the one oust the other?

After all, this is not some new thing. The Anglican-Roman Catholic Commission did not introduce this. It has been there all the time. Since the Prayer Book, this ceremony has predicated Infant Regeneration by the priestly sacrament of water. In other words, that water imparts Christ. What have evangelicals had to say about this? They have pointed confidently to the articles, particularly the article on justification.

Strange dichotomy. On the one hand, fervently preaching justification by faith only through the gospel in a way of rational belief. On the other hand, actually practising regeneration by sacramental water through the priesthood without any belief at all.

Must not the one of necessity cancel out the other? Which is it to be? The articles of theoretic doctrine or the rite of actual practice? Well, in the vast majority of cases, which is it?

One may object, But the articles define the gospel. The sacraments confirm belief in that gospel.

First, we do not accept that the articles *define* the gospel although it is certainly true that they contain many excellent aphorisms. Next, we repudiate categorically the word and notion 'sacrament', as being in defiance of the holy apostles and the doctrine of Christ.*   Third, the 'sacraments' cannot confirm the 'belief' of a non-voluntary infant incapable of hearing, knowing, or doing anything about what is being perpetrated by adults over its infantile head. The baby has neither rational hearing nor voluntary will. He is incapable of faith. The 'sacrament' cannot confirm what is non-existent. Then what is its purpose?

What the baptismal 'sacrament' proposes to do in fact is to *by-pass* faith; and to *by-pass* the gospel. It does this by putting the priestly rite in place of faith, by putting water in place of the gospel, and by putting an uncomprehending infant in place of a believer. What it declares in fact is this: 'WATER IMPARTS CHRIST.' Otherwise, why do it?

But we declare the holy scriptures with Christ and his holy apostles, NOTHING BUT THE GOSPEL IMPARTS CHRIST.

* See 'The Messiah', the 4th beatitude, particularly pages 201-204.

Indeed the real issue of the Reformation — at its most aware and intelligent — never was about the virtue and merits of Christ's person nor his sacrifice on Calvary. The real issue, the burning issue, was this: GIVEN THOSE MERITS, HOW ARE THEY IMPUTED AND HIS PERSON IMPARTED?

The Church of England Articles declared 'by faith only.' Justification by faith only. That was at the heart of the Reformation. Not the justification so much as the imputing of justification. 'By faith only.' But this is what the baptismal rite in the same Church of England Prayer Book flatly contradicts. 'By water also.' And since — just as infancy precedes maturity — the water came before the faith, the ultimate issue could never be in doubt. Why? Because the water rendered the faith superfluous. The baptismal rite claimed already to have done the work. If so, it dispenses with faith.

But once reverse the process, and declare that justification is by faith only, then that sacramental system which dispenses with faith is seen as one which actually disposes of justification. In effect, it is as perfect a system of condemnation as human ingenuity and diabolical subtlety could ever devise.

The error lies in the presumption that the gospel and the means of communicating it are two separate things. That the virtue and merits of Christ are defined as one thing and the imparting of those virtues and merits as another thing altogether. They are not. Both these things are one in the gospel. The gospel includes in itself how it is communicated.

The means of communication, the method of imparting, are contained within the gospel. It is part of the gospel, equally to be believed. Divide Christ from the way in which he is imparted; separate Christ's merits from the way in which they are communicated; then you have a mutilation, a perversion, not the gospel. But if you have the gospel, and believe it, the thing is done in and of itself. This is called 'justification by faith only'.

This is what we have been stressing: Nothing but the gospel imparts Christ. That is, the means of conveying all the benefits and merits of Christ and his work are within the gospel. Believe that gospel, and they are conveyed.

There is no doubt that since the Reformation to the present time evangelical clergymen have been stressing this self-same thing. In word. But in works they do the opposite. Every Anglican clergyman must practise what gives the lie to justification by faith only. Namely, that justification is by water also. Every time a baby is christened the priest practically declares that water imparts Christ. The sacramental priesthood has 'Christ-ened' the baby: made it 'regenerate ... grafted into the body of Christ's church.' Yet withal these works at the font, from the pulpit the words of evangelical clergymen have energetically declared 'justification by faith only.'

There could be but one conclusion to this compromising contradiction.

And now that conclusion has come to pass.

As to what has come to pass, let the evangelical

clergymen, leaders of evangelicals from all denominations and in all conventions, let them speak for themselves. Hear the one-time curate from All Souls, Langham Place, for example, now an Evangelical Anglican tutor of the priesthood himself. Seven years under the respected evangelical leader, Rev. John Stott he served, whom evangelicals from all walks delight to follow. Let us see where he has taken us all.

I give quotations from the pamphlet of the Rev. Julian Charley, evangelical member of the Anglican-Roman Catholic Commission. In turn he quotes from the recommendations of the commission itself, in love inviting us all to concur and participate. My own comments follow each quotation.

> *'THE AGREED ROMAN CATHOLIC-CHURCH OF ENGLAND STATEMENT OF EUCHARISTIC DOCTRINE.*
>
> *'III, THE PRESENCE OF CHRIST.'*

What he is saying is, The presence of Christ *in the bread and wine*. He is saying that.

> *'PARA. 7. Christ is present and active in various ways in the entire eucharistic celebration.'*

What he means is, Christ is present and active in the Sacrificial Priest (who may or may not be an 'Evangelical' like himself); present and active in the sacrificial bread;

present and active in the sacrificial wine. Present and active generally. 'Various ways.' In these various ways Christ is imparted through bread and wine. He says.

> *'Christ who through his minister presides*
> *at the table ... gives himself sacramentally*
> *in the body and blood of his paschal*
> *sacrifice.'*

In other words the body and blood of Jesus, slain on Calvary, are claimed mystically to infuse the bread and wine when the sacrificial priest makes consecration at the altar-table, so that this bread and wine become transubstantiated or consubstantiated into *the very same sacrifice made at Calvary, two thousand years ago. This is then fed to the people.*

And our evangelical leader is telling us that it is quite all right for us to accept this that has come to pass. That is what the evangelical clergyman believes.

Well, now you know what has come to pass.

The Mass has come to pass.

> *'PARA. 8. The sacramental body and*
> *blood of the Saviour are present as an*
> *offering ... in order to be the Lord's real*
> *gift of himself to his church.'*

Here you see that the bread and wine are transubstantiated so that they *really become* or at least *contain as actually present* the body and blood of the Saviour. Only in

36

this way does the Lord make a *real* gift of himself to the church.

Then Calvary alone was an incomplete gift? Then faith in the blood and sacrifice at Calvary is an unreal faith in an incomplete gift? Then the gospel on its own does not convey Christ neither his blood nor his flesh? No; according to this evangelical and the Commission, that is unreal.

It is only real under the Authority of the first bishop of Rome; that is, the Pope. Only real when consecrated by the new Anglican-Roman Catholic Ministry; that is, the priesthood. Only real when it is completed as a real gift by the offering of the same sacrifice in the Eucharist; that is, the Mass. Then it is real. Otherwise, it is intangible. Unreal. So incomplete as to be incommunicable.

This is the pass to which our evangelical leaders have brought us. And this is but the beginning of the end!

Nevertheless, beginning or no, it is still the Mass.

> *'PARA. 9. The elements are not mere signs. Christ's body and blood become really present and are really given.'*

Is it not the Mass? Now can we not see why Knox cried — as men knelt to bread and wine and worshipped them, supposing that the priest had turned them into Christ — Knox cried in horror: 'That idol, the Mass!'

> *'PARA. 10. According to the traditional order of the liturgy ... the bread and wine*

> *become the body and blood of Christ by*
> *the action of the Holy Spirit, so that in*
> *communion we eat the flesh of Christ and*
> *drink his blood.'*

Here there is no pretence of claiming scriptural support for the liturgical position of the 'eucharist'. And if not, then no claim for apostolic origin and authority. The claim is to tradition alone: 'according to the traditional order of the liturgy.' There is no scriptural order. When this first was invented the scripture had closed and the apostles were long dead. Then arose this tradition of the sacramental mass and priesthood, contradictory both to the scriptural doctrine and the apostolic ordinance. Otherwise what further need was there for a tradition to arise, contrary to that which had been delivered already by the apostolic commandment? But this true authority the Commission ignores, as it must, and for its neo-mass can only appeal to 'the traditional order of the liturgy.'

Now then hear the word of the Lord: 'He answered and said unto them, Well hath Esaias prophesied of you hypocrites, as it is written, This people honoureth me with their lips, but their heart is far from me.

'Howbeit in vain do they worship me, teaching for doctrines the commandments of men.

'For laying aside the commandment of God, ye hold the tradition of men ...

'And he said unto them, Full well ye reject the commandment of God, that ye may keep your own tradition.'

But the temerity of this new tradition puts into the shade anything dared by the impiety of the elders, scribes and Pharisees of the Jews. For what does the Commission dare to say of the Holy Spirit? 'The bread and wine become the body and blood of Christ by the action of the Holy Spirit ... in communion.' Wherever does it say so? In all the references in the scriptures to the person and work of the Holy Ghost, tell me, Where is the remotest hint of any such suggestion? There is none. None at all. I defy them to deny it: there is not a shadow, a hint, from any apostle or in all the Holy Bible to suggest any such thing. Then how dare they say it?

Verily I say unto you, this exceeds the temerity of the elders who set aside the word of God by their traditions. This tradition not only sets aside the word of God. It sets aside the Spirit of God himself. For by their tradition they take the Holy Ghost from his chosen place in scripture and make him the servant and steward of a system totally opposed to the gospel and utterly alien to the Holy Bible.

Moreover — so far as in them lies — neither has Christ fared any better at their hands. For whilst nominally admitting that Christ Jesus is the one mediator between God and men, practically they take him from all mankind and all mankind from him by interposing their own mediation. So that he is not really accessible but by their priesthood, any more than Jehovah was accessible but by the Levitical priesthood.

However the apostles taught us that Christ had come to do away with all human interposition, and, taking the priestly order into his own hands, to call all mankind directly to himself without any intermediary, saying, Whosoever shall call on the name of the Lord shall be saved. And, The word is nigh thee, even in thy mouth, and in thy heart: that is, the word of faith, which we preach: That if thou shalt confess with thy mouth the Lord Jesus, and shalt believe in thine heart that God hath raised him from the dead, thou shalt be saved. Romans 10:8, 9. Then, where is their mediatorial priesthood?

Not only do they take Christ from us and us from Christ, but they make him inaccessible save through their sacramental ministrations. Furthermore, they wrench Christ's finished work on Calvary out of his own hands. Not content with all this, finally they steal his complete gospel away from him. They make him — so far as in them lies — dependent upon themselves and their eucharistic offering in order actually to convey his sacrifice to those who cry out to him in their need. He cannot reach them and they cannot reach him. No, the sacramental ministry must bridge the impassable gulf.

No more will they allow Jesus' sacrifice at Calvary to be adequate or effectual. Only the Roman Authorised Priesthood can work the necessary change upon the bread and wine to make the sacrifice complete, and make it good to all who receive it at their hands. Otherwise it were an incomplete sacrifice unable to reach mankind. Without their sacramental ministration it could not be 'the Lord's real gift of himself to the church.' It could only be a gift suspended from heaven out of reach of common man, but nevertheless within reach of that priestly ministry authorised by the first bishop of Rome.

Since we are informed that the arm of Christ is shortened that it cannot save, that is, that it cannot quite reach to man, therefore we are dependent upon this ministry to grasp the sacrifice from Christ's outstretched but shortened arm. Thus this priesthood must bridge the gap from him to humanity, transubstantiating bread and wine into flesh and blood to close the circuit.

If this is not insulting and degrading Christ, what is? If this is not telling lies in the name of the Lord, what is telling lies in the name of the Lord? If this is not diminishing and belittling the work of Christ, what is?

Behold these enemies of the Lord and his gospel! Mark them narrowly, for they are not above transforming themselves into angels of light and ministers of righteousness. Already by fair words they have deceived the simple. By their sleight of hand, and by the cunning craftiness whereby they have lain in wait to deceive, many have been ensnared and have had their eyesight taken away, much as the Philistines caught Samson, afterwards putting out his eyes.

But the eyesalve we have obtained of Christ, and the apostolic ministry that has opened countless eyes before ours and now causes the radiance of the gospel to break in upon us, speaketh on this wise: That a man is justified by faith without works. And if without works, then without the works of the first bishop of Rome. Without the works of his priesthood. Without the works of his sacraments. And without the works of his church.

He that believeth is justified freely by grace through faith in Christ alone. God has set him forth to be a propitiation through faith in his blood. It is nothing whatever to do with the church. Nor the sacramental ministry. It is the work of God alone. 'This is the work of God that ye believe.'

In this way of faith righteousness of God is freely imputed unto all and upon all them that believe. There are no intermediaries; there is nothing to do; nothing is to be added; it is one gift once and for all. Christ is the end of the law for righteousness to every one that believeth. Believe on the Lord Jesus Christ and thou shalt be saved, and thy house. I tell you, NOTHING BUT THE GOSPEL IMPARTS CHRIST. And nothing but faith receives him.

Then how have we got to the pass that we have?

It is due entirely to the leaders that have led evangelicals now for some generations, and increasingly to the present time. At the first they flattered and were in alliance with liberals of the modernistic school from Germany, thinking themselves very daring. But now, like the prodigal son, any company at all will do, provided only that it does not include any of the remaining spiritual brethren. Nor, above all, some Elijah who — unknown to them — the Spirit of the Lord has hidden away even for such a time as this.

And what shall such an Elijah cry to them in the word of the Lord? Why, this:

> They are that stubborn and rebellious generation; a generation that set not their heart aright, and whose spirit was not steadfast with God.

42

> They are the children of Ephraim who,
> being armed, and carrying bows, turned
> back in the day of battle.

Psalm 78.

That is them. And what saith the word of the Lord of them?

> Curse ye Meroz, said the angel of the
> LORD, curse ye bitterly the inhabitants
> thereof; because they came not to the
> help of the LORD, to the help of the
> LORD against the mighty.

What is a thousand times worse is this: it is not that they are liberals, or modernist unbelievers themselves. Not at all. It is not that they are Romans or perform the sacerdotal rite of the Mass for the Roman Pontiff. That has not happened yet in the Church of England. No. They are evangelicals. They lead the conventions. They lead the evangelistic meetings. They lead the missions. The free church ministers are thrilled to share the platform with these evangelical clergymen. The brethren are flattered. They lead evangelicalism in fact. But it is their church which has published this Agreement. An agreement with the Pope, the Mass and the sacrificial priesthood. And it is one of their number, an evangelical, who sat on that Committee. Stott's protégé, Julian Charley.

These things being so I observe a dreadful truism. Today it takes nothing but a neo-evangelical to achieve what flattery, persecution, wealth, poverty, life, death, blood, fire, bribes, prison, sword and the gallows could never achieve with our forefathers. And what is this that it takes them to achieve?

It takes an 'evangelical' to lead the deluded into thinking that one can profess the gospel, and at the same time condone papist practices that deny it.

It takes an 'evangelical' still to pretend the faith he actually sets aside, still to preach the word his practice really denies, still to uphold a position that he no more occupies than did Simon Magus. It takes this evangelical to cry 'All one in Christ Jesus;' 'None but Jesus;' 'Jesus Christ is Lord;' from the rooftops, yet remain strangely silent about the ghastly blow struck at the Authority of Christ by Popery; the blasphemous insult to the Holy Ghost perpetrated by the Mass; the miserable overturning of the gospel of God by the admission of a sacerdotal clergy.

It takes an 'evangelical' to lead the evangelicals right back to the Holy Father, to the Vatican, and to the Mass itself, and agree to tell us that this is all right. All right to own one common priestly and episcopal authority under the 'Chief among equals'.

All right to set up a universal hierarchy with the ultimate intention of an exclusive monopoly dispensing the sole right and authority to minister. All right to call the sacramental Roman Priesthood 'the Ministry'. All right to 'avoid emotive language' — that is, tell lies through misrepresentation — and call the Mass the 'Eucharist'.

Oh, it takes an evangelical to explain all this. All the

Mass-Eucharist subtlety of 1971. All the Priesthood-Ministry sleight of hand in 1973. All the Pope-First-Bishop conniving of 1976. All this! Yes it takes an 'evangelical' to explain it: otherwise we simple, trusting, uncritical, confused 'laity' might misunderstand it all.

All this! Yes all this that proclaims in essence 'nothing but our authority, our episcopacy, our Pope; nothing but our church, our clergy, our ministry, our sacraments; our holy water; our mass-eucharist.' Oh above all our eucharist, authorised to be dispensed by our sole authority under the one earthly Head of the Church.

Yes it takes an evangelical, because he is so reassuring. Otherwise even led by the nose to the slaughter like fools as we have been, otherwise even *we* might stop; think; wrinkle our gullible brows: yes, and even we might cry out! For the stones cry out.

But if it is to be done a neo-evangelical is the man to do it.

For it takes an evangelical. I tell you, it takes an evangelical, and best of all one on the Roman Catholic-Church of England Commission, to cloak vicious and fundamental error with a hundred texts, a thousand subtle words, page on page of irrelevant, immaterial and inapplicable 'idealistic' utterances nothing at all to do with what is actually going on!

And what is going on? The slow, the inexorable, the patient, the long-term *gathering of force*. What force? Force to demand universal agreement that Christ is conveyed

45

solely by their eucharist, through their ministry, under their first bishop. It takes an evangelical to do that. Afterwards, he will drop the cloak. But now he takes it up, he wraps it round. He is an 'evangelical', you see. Because evangelicals would follow no one else.

Follow him where? Well, wherever he is going. Trace with me his journey. It is not done yet.

Not done yet, but only an 'evangelical' could have got so far. Only he could so softly draw the bewitched and hypnotised evangelicals. But he has.

It takes an evangelical to wade through the blood of ten thousand martyrs who in their day died because they would not *hear*, much less *do* the proposals of the Agreement urged on us by the evangelicals. But then those martyrs lived in their Bibles. And in total contrast for a hundred years and more evangelicalism has been yielding, giving, softening, compromising. And it is hard to change now, isn't it? So easy to follow.

Oh, it takes an 'evangelical' to beckon the evangelistic crowd, the convention multitude, the free brethren, all to follow suit, ignoring their bloody and soaking legs. It takes an evangelical to scatter the ashes, to brush aside the bones, of Latimer, Ridley, Tyndale and a host of faithful witnesses, to raise as clouds the dust of Englishmen who burned rather than do exactly what the Roman Catholic-Church of England Commission has done and calls upon us to do.

It takes an evangelical. He is an Anglican. But he could as easily be a Methodist, a Presbyterian, a Baptist, even some of the leading Christian Brethren today. For all we like sheep have gone astray.

But whether it takes an 'evangelical' or not — for whether they will carry us away will depend upon God and God alone — one thing is true this day: They are telling us a corrupt and soul-deceiving lie of damning consequences. This is the truth, the whole truth, and nothing but the truth:

NOTHING BUT THE GOSPEL IMPARTS CHRIST.

But these things being so, *why has there not been an outcry?* Because evangelicals do not care enough. Because the clergy, ministers, evangelists, convention committees, church rulers, are so much a clique, so looking sideways, so much in a kind of union, *that they will not stand up individually and be counted.* And if some do not agree, they would not dream of offending their Anglican and Catholic 'fellow-believers'. Rather than that, the truth is, they would prefer to offend Christ.

Oh, evangelicals cry, Don't exaggerate, don't criticise, it is nothing like that! Isn't it? Does your Bible teach you that the Holy Ghost is to be equated with incanted tap water so that *that* regenerates an infant? Does your gospel make the blood of Jesus shed on Calvary the *property* of the Roman Hierarchy which magically changes cheap Italian wine *into the priceless blood of Christ* every Sunday all over the world for two thousand years? Does your evangelicalism allow the wafer made from common grain to be turned into the *very flesh of Jesus on the cross* because some medieval rite is muttered over it by a priest? If it does, go and join them. You have neither part nor lot in the matter. Your

47

portion falls with the uncircumcised idolaters. 'He that is filthy, let him be filthy still.'

Nevertheless, let every one that nameth the name of Christ depart from iniquity. 'Depart ye, depart ye ... touch no unclean thing.'

'Come out of her, my people, that ye be not partakers of her sins.' Who is on the Lord's side, who?

Dare you shrug and say, It doesn't matter? Then hell doesn't matter. Damnation doesn't matter. Everlasting torment doesn't matter. For that is the issue. Either we receive Christ aright or we do not receive him at all. Either we continue in this only faith to the end or we cast off our first faith, make shipwreck concerning the faith, and deny the faith by subsequently falling away from the simplicity which is in Christ.

Either Christ and his merits are preached, and received by faith alone. Or a false Christ and its wafer and wine are sacrificed by the priesthood under the 'first bishop of Rome' and received by works only.

But you cannot have the two. That is not evangelical! These things are mutually exclusive. It is one or the other. For God is witness. We speak the truth and lie not. We have told you only the truth:

NOTHING BUT THE GOSPEL IMPARTS CHRIST AND NOTHING BUT FAITH RECEIVES HIM.

●　　●　　●

Please send to the address below:—

			Quantity
The Gospel of God	£0.25 +	10p	☐
The Messiah	£1.20 +	55p	☐
Noah and the Flood	£0.60 +	19p	☐
The Wells of Salvation	£0.60 +	26p	☐
The Birth of Jesus Christ	£0.45 +	15p	☐
Foundations Uncovered	£0.30 +	12p	☐
The Red Heifer	£0.25 +	12p	☐
Divine Footsteps	£0.40 +	12p	☐
The Two Prayers of Elijah	£0.10 +	7p	☐

(Additional (+) price shows postage & packing)

NAME AND ADDRESS (in block capitals)

——————————————————————

——————————————————————

——————————————————————

Enclose remittance with order.